365 Black: Nuggets of Wisdom
for each day of the year

Selected, Edited, & Arranged by
Lathardus Goggins II. Ed.D.

Saint Rest Publications
Akron, OH

ISBN 978-0-9663972-3-9 (e-book)

ISBN 978-0-9663972-5-3 (paperback)

Cover design by Lathardus Goggins II, Ed.D.

Saint Rest Publications
PO Box 1852
Akron, OH 44309
http://www.afrocentric.info/SaintRest

Contents

Introduction

"What 'we' have to do is reactivate the memory of 'us.' ... and in the process of remembering is the process of Sankofa."
Dr. Marimba Ani (2008)

365 Black: Nuggets of Wisdom for Each Day of the Year is a collection of quotes, proverbs, and sayings that represent a very small sample of the collective wisdom within the African experience. This book is meant to help the reader to become aware of and connect to the wisdom forged in the African experience; a wisdom and experience often overlooked, undervalued, or assumed not to exist.

I make no claim that this collection is exhaustive or representative of the "full" experience. This collection is heavily bias towards the African-American experience. In my effort to better represent the African Diaspora, I include proverbs form 37 different African ethnics groups and countries. I have also included activist and scholars with a Pan-African perspective.

365 Black: Nuggets of Wisdom for Each Day of the Year is organized by month and date. Each day has a specific "nugget" of wisdom; some are simple one-liners while others are more lengthly. However, each is an opportunity to reflect on a thought/idea/value rooted in African cultural heritage.

To reflect think about:

- What is the main point and why is it being said?
- How does the main point impacts/guides your actions/thoughts/advocacy/relationships?
- If more people in your family/community was informed/guided by the main idea, how would your family/community change?

I hope you will share your reflections and "our" collective wisdom with your family and friends. Remember - "Each one, teach one" and Pamoja tutashinda (Together we will succeed)!

Lathardus Goggins II, Ed.D.

Publisher

SAINT REST PUBLICATIONS

http://www.afrocentric.info/SaintRest

JANUARY

Lift every voice and sing, Till earth and heaven ring,
Ring with the harmonies of Liberty; let our rejoicing rise
High as the listening skies, Let it resound loud as the rolling sea.
Sing a song full of the faith that the dark past has taught us,
Sing a song full of the hope that the present has brought us,
Facing the rising sun of our new day begun
Let us march on till victory is won.

Stony the road we trod, Bitter the chastening rod,
Felt in the days when hope unborn had died;
Yet with a steady beat, Have not our weary feet
Come to the place for which our fathers sighed?
We have come over a way that with tears have been watered,
We have come, treading our path through the blood of the slaughtered,
Out from the gloomy past, Till now we stand at last
Where the white gleam of our bright star is cast.

God of our weary years, God of our silent tears,
Thou who has brought us thus far on the way;
Thou who has by Thy might, Led us into the light,
Keep us forever in the path, we pray.
Lest our feet stray from the places, Our God, where we met Thee;
Lest, our hearts drunk with the wine of the world, we forget Thee;
Shadowed beneath Thy hand, May we forever stand.
True to our GOD, True to our native land.

James Weldon Johnson (1900)
Lift Every Voice and Sing

1

Make yourself the subject of intense study, and you will find God.

Proverb - KMT

2

Social scientist are now convinced that children learn social, racial, and religious prejudices in the course of observing, and being influenced by, the existence of patterns in the culture in which they live.

Kenneth B. Clark, Ph.D.

3

Nothing succeeds like success.

Alexandre Dumas

4

I don't know the key to success, but the key to failure is trying to please everybody.

William (Bill) Cosby, Ed.D.

5

No act of kindness, no matter how small, is ever wasted.

Aesop

6

We must reinforce argument with results.

Booker T. Washington

7

A tree is known by its fruit.

Proverb - Zulu (South Africa)

8

It's alright to crawl before you walk; it's alright to walk before you run;
But, if you wanna get what you never got, gotta do something that you
never done.

Mary Mary (Erica Campbell / Tina Campbell / Warryn Campbell)

9

A fish is the last to acknowledge the existence of water.

Proverb - Ewe (Ghana)

10

If the integration of two groups legally and socially separated for more
than 350 years does not produce friction, it is the surest sign that no
meaningful change has taken place.

Orlando Patterson, Ph.D.

11

Great fires erupt from tiny sparks.

Proverb - Libya

12

The only protection against injustice in man is power- physical, financial, and scientific.

Marcus Garvey

13

The difference between treason and patriotism is only a matter of dates.

Alexandre Dumas

14

Stop using the word "Negro." The word is a misnomer from every point of view. It does not represent a country or anything else ... I am an African-American ... I am not ashamed of my African descent... After people have been freed, it is a cruel injustice to call them the same name they bore as slaves.

Mary Church Terrell (1949)

15

We know through painful experience that freedom is never voluntarily given by the oppressor; it must be demanded by the oppressed. Frankly, I have yet to engage in a direct action campaign that was "well timed" in the view of those who have not suffered unduly from the disease of segregation. For years now I have heard the word "Wait!" It rings in the ear of every Negro with piercing familiarity. This "Wait" has almost always meant "Never." We must come to see, with one of our distinguished jurists, that "justice too long delayed is justice denied."

Rev. Martin L. King, Jr., Ph.D.

16

One hand does not catch a buffalo.

Proverb - Ewe (Ghana)

17

I hated every minute of training, but I said, "Don't quit. Suffer now and live the rest of your life as a champion."

Muhammad Ali

18

There are many statues of men slaying lions, but if only the lions were sculptors there might be quite a different set of statues.

Aesop

19

Racism systematically verifies itself; anytime the slave can only be free by imitating his master.

Jamil Abdullah Al-Amin (H. Rap Brown)

20

When elephants fight, it's the grass that suffers.

Proverb - Ngoreme (Tanzania)

21

In a racially divided society, majority rule may become majority tyranny.

Lani Guinier, J.D.

22

Keep your place in life and your place will keep you.

Aesop

23

Provided no person destroys a sprouting palm kernel,

it will definitely grow into a palm tree.

Proverb - Esan (Nigeria)

24

The empowerment of black women constitutes ...

the empowerment of our entire community

Kimberlè Crenshaw, J.D.

25

Would America have been America without her Negro people?

W. E. B. DuBois, Ph.D.

26

When considering the impact of one's actions, intentions are amongst the least important concerns. Consider arriving at a scene of an accident. Does it matter, if the person was run over by accident or on purpose? It does not effect the treatment. Intentions only matter to the person perpetrating the harm.

Lathardus Goggins II, Ed.D.

27

It's only the mad man that goes to bed with his roof on fire.

Proverb - Nigeria

28

One who enters the forest does not enter it to listen to his own breaking twigs.

Proverb - Bemba (Zambia)

29

I freed a thousand slaves. I could have freed a thousand more if only they knew, they were slaves.

Harriet Tubman

30

Madison Avenue is afraid of the dark.

Nat King Cole

31

When I discover who I am, I'll be free.

Ralph Ellison

FEBRUARY

If you control a man's thinking, you do not have to worry about his action. When you determine what a man shall think, you do not have to concern yourself about what he will do. If you make a man feel inferior, you do not have to compel him to accept an inferior status, he will seek it himself. If you make a man think he is justly an outcast, you do not have to order him to the back door. He will go without being told; and if there is no back door, his very nature will demand one.

Dr. Carter G Woodson (1933),

The Mis-Education of the Negro

1

When there is no enemy within, the enemies outside cannot hurt you.

Proverb

2

Many demand that we "get past race." But denials of cancer, no matter how vigorous they may be, will not make the malignancy go away.

Clarence Page

3

Better be wise by the misfortunes of others than by your own.

Aesop

4

Since you was tricked, I have to raise ya; from the cradle to the grave. But remember you're not a slave; Cause we was put here to be much more than that, But we couldn't see it because our mind was trapped. But I'm here to break away the chains, take away the pains; Remake the brains.

Rakim

5

A stick is straighten while still young.

Proverb - Kiga (Uganda)

6

For colored people to acquire learning in this country
makes tyrants quake and tremble on their sandy foundation.

David Walker

7

"Go in that direction" does not mean that you go.
To go means "let's go together!"

Proverb - Sena (Mozambique)

8

Our elevation must be the result of self-efforts and work of
our own hands. No other human power can accomplish it.
If we but determine it shall be so, it will be so.

Martin Delany

9

If these town gods can't detect the thieves who steal from their own temples, it's hardly likely they'll tell me who stole my spade.

Aesop

10

Never underestimate the power of dreams and
the influence of the human spirit.

Wilma Rudolph

11

It is not so much a Negro History Week ... We should
emphasize not Negro History, but the Negro in history.

Carter G. Woodson, Ph.D.

12

A good head and good heart are always a formidable combination. But when you add to that a literate tongue or pen, then you have something very special.

Nelson Mandela

13

If my mind can conceive it,

and my heart can believe it

- then I can achieve it.

Muhammad Ali

14

True love always makes a man better,

no matter what woman inspires it.

Alexandre Dumas

15

It is the fool whose own tomatoes are sold to him.

Proverb - Akan

16

There is not a soul without sin. Yet we should strive

towards perfecting ourselves through action.

Sista Souljah

17

Those who profess to favor freedom and yet depreciate agitation are people who want crops without ploughing the ground; they want rain without thunder and lightning; they want the ocean without the roar of its many waters. The struggle may be a moral one, or it may be a physical one, or it may be both. But it must be a struggle. Power concedes nothing without a demand. It never did and it never will.

Frederick Douglass

18

If you refuse the elder's advice you will walk the whole day.

Proverb - Ngoreme (Tanzania)

19

We have to keep in mind at all times that we are not fighting for integration, nor are we fighting for separation. We are fighting for recognition as free humans in this society.

El-Hajj Malik El-Shabazz (Malcolm X)

20

Like ants, eat little and carry the rest back to your home.

Proverb - Bembe (Tanzania)

21

Our nettlesome task is to discover how to organize
our strength into compelling power.

Rev. Martin Luther King, Jr., Ph.D.

22

Molded on Africa's anvil, tempered down home.

Julian Bond

23

The main thing is the YOU beneath the clothes and skin--the ability to
do, the will to conquer, the determination to understand and know this
great, wonderful, curious world.

W.E.B. DuBois, Ph.D.

24

Beauty fades, but learning last.

Elder's wisdom

25

Every race and every nation should be judged by the
best it has been able to produce, not by the worst.

James Weldon Johnson

26

The truth is, everyone is going to hurt you.
You just got to find the ones worth suffering for.

Bob Marley

27

He who does not cultivate his field will die of hunger.

Proverb

28

If you understand the beginning well, the end will not trouble you.

Proverb

Bonus (Day 29)

The question is - Why are African people around the world, including those in the Americas, denied the greatness of their history by those who have oppressed and exploited us?

The answer is - That a people who never did anything is not likely to envision itself as doing anything. ... remember that the masses of African people in the Americas today were not brought here out of the good will. They were brought here to be exploited. It is far easier to exploit a people if they have little self-worth; and the best way to delete a people's self-worth is to deny them a great history.

Runoko Rashidi

MARCH

"That man over there says that women need to be helped into carriages, and lifted over ditches, and to have the best place everywhere. Nobody ever helps me into carriages, or over mud puddles, or gives me any best place! And, ain't I a woman? Look at me! Look at my arm! I have ploughed and planted, and gathered into barns, and no man could head me! And, ain't I a woman? I could work as much and eat as much as a man - when I could get it – and bear the lash as well! And, ain't I a woman? I have borne thirteen children, and seen most all sold off to slavery, and when I cried out with my mother's grief, none but Jesus heard me! And, ain't I a woman? ...

Then that little man in black there, he says women can't have as much rights as men, 'cause Christ wasn't a woman! Where did your Christ come from? Where did your Christ come from? From God and a woman! Man had nothing to do with Him.

If the first woman God ever made was strong enough to turn the world upside down all alone, these women together ought to be able to turn it back, and get it right side up again! And, now they is asking to do it, the men better let them."

Sojourner Truth (1851)
Ain't I A Woman?

18

1

When you bear a grudge, your child will also bear a grudge.

Proverb - Rwanda

2

By accepting and understanding our connection to Africa, we begin to love our Blackness and celebrate the essence of our beauty in its purest form: sweet, true and God-kissed.

Rita Rogers

3

Suffering is prior to attaining success or perfection.

Proverb - Chagga (Tanzania)

4

Face your fears and experience the beauty of people and places far away from your self.

Sista Souljah

5

The time has come for the Black man to forget and cast behind him his hero worship and adoration of other races ... We must canonize our own martyrs and elevate to positions of fame and honor Black men and women ... Sojourner Truth is worthy of sainthood alongside of Joan of Arc. Crispus Attucks and George William Gordon are entitled to the halo of martyrdom with no less glory than that of the martyrs of any other race.

Marcus Garvey

6

A man's mind is elevated to the status of the women with whom he associates.

Alexander Dumas

7

The eyes of a wise person see through you.

Proverb - Haya (Tanzania)

8

To our Ancestors the Black Woman was Mother Sky, Mother Earth, Mother of Everything and she had the power to, through her spiritual essence, move freely throughout the universe. They believed that man could only reach the pinnacle of his spiritual being through her. I know some insecure brothers may not like to hear this, but if you are spiritually attuned and your manhood is intact, then you will understand. And you will do, like our wise Afrikan Ancestors, you will fight to the death to defend her honor because that's where your source of power and strength comes from.

Ishakamusa Barashango

9

Dipped in chocolate, bronzed with elegance, enameled with grace, toasted with beauty. My Lord, she is a Black woman.

Yosef ben-Jochannan, Ph.D.

10

A child who is to be successful is not reared exclusively on a bed of down.

Proverb - Akan (Ghana)

11

I must oppose any attempt that Negroes may make to do to others what has been done to them ... I know the spiritual wasteland to which that road leads... whoever debases others is debasing himself.

James Baldwin

12

Justice demands integrity. It's to have a moral universe — not only know what is right or wrong but to put things in perspective, weigh things. Justice is different from violence and retribution; it requires complex accounting.

bell hooks, Ph.D.

13

Truth-tellers are not always palatable; there is a preference for candy bars.

Gwendolyn Brooks

14

Only a wise person solves difficult problems.

Proverb - Akan (Ghana)

15

A man's bread and butter is only insured when he works for it.

Marcus Garvey

16

Children learn more from what you are than what you teach.

W.E.B. DuBois, Ph.D.

17

When God cooks, you don't see the smoke.

Proverb - Kaonde (Zambia)

18

When you are being criminally mistreated, the criminal does not have right to say which tactics should be used to get him off your back.

El-Hajj Malik El-Shabazz (Malcolm X)

19

The friend of a fool is a fool. The friend of
a wise person is another wise person.

The Husia

20

A deaf ear is followed by death and
an ear that listens is followed by blessings.

Proverb - Samburu (Kenya)

21

Champions aren't made in gyms. Champions are made from something they have deep inside them-a desire, a dream, a vision. They have to have the skill, and the will. But the will must be stronger than the skill.

Muhammad Ali

22

When feminism does not explicitly oppose racism, and when antiracism does not incorporate opposition to patriarchy, race and gender politics often end up being antagonistic to each other and both interests lose.

Kimberlè Crenshaw, J.D.

23

A chattering bird builds no nest.

Proverb

24

I am an example of what is possible when girls from the very beginning of their lives are loved and nurtured by people around them. I was surrounded by extraordinary women in my life who taught me about quiet strength and dignity.

Michelle Obama, J.D.

25

When you see clouds gathering, prepare to catch rainwater.

Proverb

26

The segregation of the 90's is between the
educated haves and the uneducated have-nots.

Manning Marable, Ph.D.

27

For I am my mother's daughter, and the drums of Africa still beat in my heart. They will not let me rest while there is a single Negro boy or girl without a chance to prove his worth.

Mary McLeod Bethune

28

Everything that he [Martin Luther King, Jr.] represented, all the people whose names never made the history books, made it possible for me to stand and be who I am and take ownership of my life.

Oprah Winfrey

29

I have only just a minute; only sixty seconds in it;

Forced upon me, can't refuse it.

Didn't seek it ... didn't choose it, but it's up to me to use it.

I must suffer, if I loose it.

Give account, if I abuse it.

Just a tiny minute, but eternity is in it.

Benjamin Mays, Ph.D.

30

If you can't bear the cross, then you can't wear the crown.

Elder's wisdom

31

Living simply makes loving simple.

bell hooks, Ph.D.

APRIL

"If you allow me to live just a few years in the second half of the 20th century, I will be happy." ... Now that's a strange statement to make, because the world is all messed up. The nation is sick. ... I see God working in this period of the twentieth century in a way that men, in some strange way, are responding. ... Something is happening in our world. The masses of people are rising up. And wherever they are assembled today, whether they are in Johannesburg, South Africa; Nairobi, Kenya; Accra, Ghana; New York City; Atlanta, Georgia; Jackson, Mississippi; or Memphis, Tennessee -- the cry is always the same: "We want to be free." ... We don't have to argue with anybody. We don't have to curse and go around acting bad with our words. We don't need any bricks and bottles. We don't need any Molotov cocktails. We just need to go ... and say, "God sent us by here, to say to you that you're not treating his children right. And we've come by here to ask you to make the first item on your agenda fair treatment, where God's children are concerned. Now, if you are not prepared to do that, we do have an agenda that we must follow. And our agenda calls for withdrawing economic support from you." ... Well, I don't know what will happen now. We've got some difficult days ahead. But it really doesn't matter with me now, because I've been to the mountaintop. And I don't mind. Like anybody, I would like to live a long life.

Longevity has its place. But I'm not concerned about that now. I just want to do God's will. And He's allowed me to go up to the mountain. And I've looked over. And I've seen the Promised Land. I may not get there with you. But I want you to know tonight, that we, as a people, will get to the promised land! And so I'm happy, tonight. I'm not worried about anything. I'm not fearing any man! Mine eyes have seen the glory of the coming of the Lord!!

Rev. Dr. Martin Luther King, Jr. (1968)

"I've Been to the Mountaintop"

1

The horse that arrives early gets good drinking water.

Proverb - Zulu

2

I am not anti-white, because I understand that white people, like black ones, are victims of a racist society. They are products of their time and place.

Shirley Chisholm

3

I don't sing song unless I feel it. The song don't tug at my heart, I pass on it. I have to believe in what I'm doing.

Ray Charles

4

A man who won't die for something is not fit to live.

Rev. Martin Luther King, Jr., Ph.D.

5

At the bottom of education, at the bottom of politics, even at the bottom of religion, there must be economic independence.

Booker T. Washington

6

When you educate a woman, you educate a nation.

Proverb - Fanti (Ghana)

7

The person who has not traveled widely thinks that her mother is the only good cook.

Proverb - Ganda (Uganda)

8

Impossible is just a big word thrown around by small men who find it easier to live in the world they've been given than to explore the power they have to change it. Impossible is not a fact. It's an opinion. Impossible is not a declaration. It's a dare. Impossible is potential. Impossible is temporary. Impossible is nothing.

Muhammad Ali

9

The most important thing to remember is this: To be ready at any moment to give up what you are for what you might become.

W. E. B. DuBois, Ph.D.

10

The whole world opened to me when I learned to read.

Mary McLeod Bethune

11

For to be free is not merely to cast off one's chains, but to live in a way that respects and enhances the freedom of others.

Nelson Mandela

12

Let the words you speak create the life you live.

Elder's wisdom

13

It takes a whole village to raise a child.

Proverb - Igbo and Yoruba (Nigeria)

14

Genuine love is rarely an emotional space where needs are instantly gratified. To know love we have to invest time and commitment... dreaming that love will save us, solve all our problems or provide a steady state of bliss or security only keeps us stuck in wishful fantasy, undermining the real power of the love -- which is to transform us.

bell hooks, Ph.D.

15

It's a hard world, I know. But don't give in to the lies.
You have always been a star; everything you need is inside. ...
Riches may come and go, only Love is pure gold.

Earth, Wind, and Fire

16

Do not count your chickens before they are hatched.

Aesop

17

Power in defense of freedom is greater than
power in behalf of tyranny and oppression.

El-Hajj Malik El-Shabazz (Malcolm X)

18

If you get a fine harvest don't break
your local brotherhood and sisterhood.

Proverb - Bembe (Tanzania)

19

We have to give our children, especially black boys, something to lose.
Children make foolish choices when they have nothing to lose.

Jawanza Kunjufu, Ed.D.

20

You must treat the earth well. It was not given to you
by your parents. It is loaned to you by your children.

Proverb - Kikuyu (Kenya)

21

The quest for Black identity involves self-respect and self-regard;
inseparable from, yet not identical to, political power and economic status.

Cornel West, Ph.D.

22

Money and success don't change people;
they merely amplify what is already there.

Will Smith

23

Be skilled in speech so that you will succeed. The tongue of a
man is his sword and effective speech is stronger that all fighting.

The Husia

24

No person is your friend who demands your silence,
or denies your right to grow.

Alice Walker

25

Rain beats a leopard's skin, but it does not wash out the spots.

Proverb

26

Men may not get all they pay for in this world,
but they must certainly pay for all they get.

Frederick Douglass

27

Men who are earnest are not afraid of consequences.

Marcus Garvey

28

Knowledge is like a garden: if it is not cultivated, it cannot be harvested.

Proverb

29

Face the world with your true face.

Sista Souljah

30

Mastery of language affords remarkable power.

Frantz Fanon

MAY

Whenever you and I are discussing our problems we need to be very objective, very cool, calm, collected. But that doesn't mean we should always be. There's a time to be cool and a time to be hot. See, you got messed up into thinking that there's only one time for everything. There's a time to love and a time to hate. ... I am not a racist in any form whatsoever. I don't believe in any form of racism. I don't believe in any form of discrimination or segregation.... But when you just judge a man because of the color of his skin, then you're committing a crime, because that's the worst kind of judgment. ... When they start indicting us because of our color that means we're indicted before we're born, which is the worst kind of crime that can be committed. ...This is a society whose government doesn't hesitate to inflict the most brutal form of punishment and oppression upon dark-skinned people all over the world. ... what's going on in and around Saigon and Hanoi and in the Congo and elsewhere. They are violent when their interests are at stake. But all of that violence that they display at the international level, when you and I want just a little bit of freedom, we're supposed to be nonviolent. They're violent. They're violent in Korea, they're violent in Germany, they're violent in the South Pacific, they're violent in Cuba, they're violent wherever they go. But when it comes time for you and me to protect ourselves against lynchings, they tell us to be nonviolent.

... "Don't struggle -- only within the ground rules that the people you're struggling against have laid down."... this is insane! ... I'm for the brotherhood of everybody, ... Long as we practice brotherhood among ourselves, and then others who want to practice brotherhood with us.

El-Hajj Malik El-Shabazz (Malcolm X) (1965)

Speech at Ford Auditorium

1

We begin by being foolish and we become wise by experience.

Proverb - Maasai (Kenya)

2

Violence is black children going to school for 12 years
and receiving 6 years worth of education.

Julian Bond

3

One important key to success is self-confidence.
An important key to self-confidence is preparation.

Arthur Ashe

4

No race can prosper till it learns that there is as
much dignity in tilling a field as in writing a poem.

Booker T. Washington

5

It is easy to be brave from a safe distance.

Aesop

6

And that is why I say to you that, though it be a thrilling and marvelous thing to be merely young and gifted in such times, it is doubly so, doubly dynamic—to be young, gifted and black. Look at the world that awaits you! Write if you will: but write about the world as it is and as you think it ought to be and must be—if there is to be a world, the beginning of writing and talking—but write to a point. Work hard at it, care about it. Write about our people: tell their story. You have something glorious to draw on - begging for attention. Don't pass it up. Use it. Good luck to you. This Nation needs your gifts. Perfect them!

Lorraine Hansberry

7

Unless you call out, who will open the door?

Proverb

8

Afrocentricity [African-centered] is the placing of African ideals at the center of any analysis that involves African culture and behavior.

Molefi Kete Asante, Ph.D.

9

How easy is it to defeat people who do not kindle fire for themselves?

Proverb - Tugen (Kenya)

10

Every great dream begins with a dreamer. Always remember, you have within you the strength, the patience, and the passion to reach for the stars to change the world.

Harriet Tubman

11

When you are playing with a dog,

do not ever forget to keep a stick within reach.

Proverb

12

You can't teach what you don't know; you can't lead where you won't go.

Jesse Jackson, Sr.

13

No matter how long a log lies in the river, it will never become a crocodile.

Proverb

14

He who starts behind in the great race of life must forever remain behind or run faster than the man in front.

Benjamin Mays, Ph.D.

15

Strategy is better than strength.

Proverb - Hausa

16

The doctrine that submission to violence is the best cure for violence did not hold good as between slaves and overseers. He was whipped oftener who was whipped easiest.

Frederick Douglass

17

Unity is strength.

Proverb - Ganda (Uganda)

18

It cannot be taken for granted that Negroes will
adhere to nonviolence under any and all conditions.

Rev. Martin Luther King, Jr., Ph.D.

19

We declare our right on this earth to be a man, to be a human being, to
respected as a human being, to be given the rights of a human being in
this society, on this earth, in this day which we intend to bring into
existence by any means necessary!

El-Hajj Malik El-Shabazz (Malcolm X)

20

Malcolm X articulated Black rage in a manner unprecedented in
American history... The substance of what he said highlighted the
chronic refusal of most Americans to acknowledge the sheer absurdity
that confronts human beings of African descent in this country - the
incessant assaults on Black intelligence, beauty, character, and
possibility.

Cornel West, Ph.D.

21

I'm sick and tired of being sick and tired.

Fannie Lou Hamer

22

Today can be a day full of excuses and regrets, or it can be a day full of progress and achievement. The choice is completely up to you.

Eric B. Turner, Ph.D.

23

This is our country! We don't have to slip around like peons or thieves in the middle of the night, asking someone for "open says me." Knock the damn door down!

Harold Washington

24

Revolution is a serious thing, the most serious thing about a revolutionary's life. When one commits oneself to the struggle, it must be for a lifetime.

Angela Davis

25

So realize, united we stand, divided we fall ... W. E. B. DuBois and Booker T, King and X, Farrakhan and Jesse; Men with means that differ, but their goals were equal - to uplift African people.

Def Jef

26

We have a powerful potential in our youth, and we must have the courage to change old ideas and practices so that we may direct their power toward good ends.

Mary McLeod Bethune

27

Do not look where you fell, but where you slipped.

Proverb

28

In the United Sates, on paper at least, the Constitution and Bill of Rights gave all Americans certain rights, including the vote and the right to be treated equally before the law. The [Civil Rights] Movement was about making those rights more than a piece of paper.

Project Hip-Hop

29

If you don't stand for something, you will fall for anything.

Proverb

30

The first need of a free people is to define their own terms.

Kwame Tourè (Stokely Carmichael)

31

When spider webs unite, they can tie up a lion.

Proverb - Ethiopia

JUNE

We have to be able to arise above our original circumstance, create place out of no place, and way out of no way, and something out of what looks originally like nothing. Let's look at the pre–creation and see if we can imitate God in that way ... Be a place–maker. Take the models in history that made a place. Listen to that. The place made by the Creator is place making because He made place out of no place. There was no place for Him; He made place. He didn't whine about the darkness ... [He] perceived infinity and projected it out and differentiated himself [from it] ... Place making. Frederick Douglass, in his autobiography of slavery said that there is no place for blacks to learn to read and write, so he creates a place. Nat Turner, place–maker; There's no place for a Black man in the halls of slavery to take off his chains and put them around his oppressor's neck. Nat Turner place–makes. He don't ask for a key, he kicks the door in. Malcolm X, place making. He didn't wait for some outside force to tell him what man is ... He makes a place for himself ... That was his criteria for manhood, waking up. Place-make Black man. You'll see how beautiful your life is.

Dr. Maulana Karenga (1995)

Black Male Think Tank

1

When you know who his friend is, you know who he is.

Proverb

2

Young single black men can either represent a positive progressive force or one that just continues to react to crisis after crisis.

Haki R. Madhubuti

3

In Africa, there are no niggers; and I will die before I become a nigger for your entertainment.

Vernon Reid

4

Culture is to human as water is to fish.

Wade Nobles, Ph.D.

5

One falsehood spoils a thousand truths.

Proverb - Ashanti (Ghana)

6

A lot of people are waiting for Martin Luther King or Mahatma Gandhi to come back - but they are gone. We are it. It is up to us. It is up to you.

Marian Wright Edelman

7

I shall neither fawn nor cringe before any party, nor stoop to beg . . . I am here to demand my rights, and to hurl thunderbolts at the men who would dare to cross the threshold of my manhood.

Henry McNeal Turner

8

He who conceals his disease cannot expect to be cured.

Proverb - Ethiopia

9

Excellence is not an act but a habit.
Things you do most are the things you do the best.

Marva Collins

10

It seems impossible until it's done.

Nelson Mandela

11

Suffering is prior to attaining success or perfection.

Proverb - Chagga (Tanzania)

12

He who is not courageous enough to take risks
will accomplish nothing in life.

Muhammad Ali

13

African-centered study is not a matter of color. It looks at any information involving African people and raises questions that allows Africans to be subjects of historical experiences rather than objects on the fringes of another's experience. ... When we center each ethnic group in their own historical and cultural experiences, we expand our knowledge of and appreciation of the human experience.

Paul Hill, Jr.

14

When you follow in the path of your father, you learn to walk like him.

Proverb - Ashanti (Ghana)

15

I see in my daughter's eyes that I am the truth.

Common

16

Strive to make something of yourself;

then strive to make the most of yourself.

Alexander Crummell

17

Once upon a time black male "cool" was defined by the ways in which black men confronted hardships of life without allowing their spirits to be ravaged. They took the pain of it and used it alchemically to turn the pain into gold. That burning process required high heat. Black male cool was defined by the ability to withstand the heat and remain centered. It was defined by black male willingness to confront reality, to face the truth, and bear it not by adopting a false pose if cool while feeding on fantasy; not by black male denial or by assuming a "poor me" victim identity. It was defined by individual black males daring to self-define rather than be defined by others.

bell hooks, Ph.D.

18

When a king has good counselors, his reign is peaceful.

Proverb - Ashanti (Ghana)

19

Patience can cook a stone.

Proverb - Fulfulde (Benin)

20

May not be able to save the whole world,

but I can save the world around me.

Otis "Big O" Gamble

21

Up, up you mighty race! You can accomplish what you will.

Marcus Garvey

22

When I discover who I am, I'll be free.

Ralph Ellison

23

What would be any more correct for any people

than to see with their own eyes?

Molefi Kete Asante, Ph.D.

24

Life is one big road with lots of signs. So when you riding through the ruts, don't complicate your mind. Flee from hate, mischief and jealousy. Don't bury your thoughts, put your vision to reality.
Wake Up and Live!

Bob Marley

25

Truth is proper and beautiful in all times and in all places.

Frederick Douglass

26

Don't be an educated fool.

Elder's wisdom

27

The root function of language is to control the universe by describing it.

James Baldwin

28

We have to constantly critique imperialist white supremacist patriarchal culture because it is normalized by mass media and rendered unproblematic.

bell hooks, Ph.D.

29

Had it not been for our art and our culture, when all else was ripped from us, we would never been able to survive as a people.

Harry Belafonte

30

You can't declare war on the Black man without declaring war on me!

Sista Souljah

JULY

This, for the purpose of this celebration, is the Fourth of July. It is the birthday of your National Independence, and of your political freedom. This, to you, as what the Passover was to the emancipated people of God ....Oppression makes a wise man mad....The 4th of July is the first great fact in your nation's history-the very ringbolt in the chain of your yet undeveloped destiny. Pride and patriotism, not less than gratitude, prompt you to celebrate and to hold it in perpetual remembrance. I have said that the Declaration of Independence is the ringbolt to the chain of your nation's destiny; so, indeed, I regard it. The principles contained in that instrument are saving principles. Stand by those principles, be true to them on all occasions, in all places, against all foes, and at whatever cost.... Fellow- citizens, pardon me, allow me to ask, why am I called upon to speak here to-day? What have I, or those I represent, to do with your national independence? ... I hear the mournful wail of millions!... What, to the American slave, is your 4th of July? I answer; a day that reveals to him, more than all other days in the year, the gross injustice and cruelty to which he is the constant victim. To him, your celebration is a sham ... This Fourth July is yours, not mine. You may rejoice, I must mourn. To drag a man in fetters into the grand illuminated temple of liberty, and call upon him to join you in joyous anthems, were inhuman mockery and sacrilegious irony.

Frederick Douglass (1852) - The Meaning of July Fourth for the Negro

1

You must judge a man by the work of his hands.

Proverb

2

Regardless of form, prejudice backed by power
deprives another person of his or her rights.

Muhammad Ali

3

Education is the primary tool of emancipation and liberation for
African-Americans in our fight for true equality in this country.

Earl G. Graves

4

Be not discourage. There is a future for you... The resistance encountered
now predicates hope ... Only as we rise ... do we encounter opposition.

Frederick Douglass

5

All lies die, when the truth is told.

Proverb

6

Our silences in the face of racist assault are acts of complicity.

bell hooks, Ph.D.

7

The tribe of "I will do it" was overtaken without having done it.

Proverb - Kenya

8

If we have the courage and tenacity of our forebears who stood firmly like a rock against the lash of slavery, we shall find a way to do for our day what they did for theirs.

Mary McLeod-Bethune

9

Racism was not just a black problem. It was America's problem. And until the country solved it, I was not going to let bigotry make me a victim instead of a full human being.

Gen. Colin Powell

10

Speak the truth, even if your voice shakes.

Elder's Wisdom

11

The experience of women and people of color is the experience of the miner's canary ... The lesson of affirmative action was that the problem is in the canary, and the solution was to fix the canary. I want to move from fixing the canary to fixing the atmosphere in the mines.

Lani Guinier, J.D.

12

Throughout history it has been the inaction of those who could have acted, the indifference of those who should have known better, the silence of the voice of justice when it mattered most that has made it possible for evil to triumph.

Haile Selassie I

13

Success is a predetermined and worthwhile goal.

Elder's Wisdom

14

As long as the mind is enslaved the body can never be free. Psychological freedom and a firm sense of self-esteem is the most powerful weapon against the long night of physical slavery.

Rev. Martin L. King, Jr., Ph.D.

15

Because we have forgotten our ancestors
our children no longer give us honor.

Maya Angelou

16

The enemy prepares a grave, but God prepares you a way of escape.

Proverb - Rwanda

17

Sometimes you have to both plan your work and work your plan.

Esi Bryant

18

I am fundamentally an optimist. Whether that comes from nature or nurture, I cannot say. Part of being optimistic is keeping one's head pointed toward the sun, one's feet moving forward. There were many dark moments when my faith in humanity was sorely tested, but I would not and could not give myself up to despair. That way lays defeat and death.

Nelson Mandela

19

It's a stirring fact that our slave ancestors left behind not documents of property but an incredible amount of cultural wealth. It is a tragedy that we are only able to imagine their individual contributions to that collective wealth- and the worlds they might have made had they been free.

Henry Louis Gates, Jr., Ph.D.

20

An elephant does not die of one broken rib.

Proverb - South Africa

21

Cunning does not last for a year.

Proverb - South Africa

22

No race has ever risen out the shadows into the sunlight without fierce opposition. ... but we shall win in the end, for we shall have God and justice and fair play on our side.

Booker T. Washington

23

The lion does not turn around when a small dog barks.

Proverb

24

The 'our-society-is-racist-and-everyone-is-guilty-Blacks-as-well-as-whites' theme is very like the 'man's-inhumanity-to-man' theme, and, like it, it excuses inhumanity by making it too universal to overcome. ... Of course, this universalization of blame implies that people of color must suffer discrimination without hope of escape.

Clarence J. Munford, Ph.D.

25

There is no difference between mother and
baby snakes; they are equally poisonous.

Proverb - Kenya

26

We cannot discuss the state of our minorities until we first have some sense of what we are, who we are, what our goals are, and what we take life to be. The question is not what we can do now for the hypothetical Mexican, the hypothetical Negro. The question is what we really want out of life, for ourselves, what we think is real.

James Baldwin

27

One's work may be finished someday, but one's education - never.

Alexandre Dumas

28

The cost of Liberty is less than the price of repression.

W. E. B. DuBois, Ph.D.

29

You have two ears and one mouth; Listen twice much than you talk.

Elders' wisdom

30

I would fight for my liberty so long as my strength lasted, and if the time came for me to go, the Lord would let them take me.

Harriet Tubman

31

God is sharper than a razor.

Proverb - Kenya

AUGUST

I am happy to join with you today in what will go down in history as the greatest demonstration for freedom in the history of our nation. ... Five score years ago, a great American, in whose symbolic shadow we stand today, signed the Emancipation Proclamation. This momentous decree came as a great beacon light of hope to millions of Negro slaves who had been seared in the flames of withering injustice. It came as a joyous daybreak to end the long night of their captivity. ... But one hundred years later, the Negro still is not free. One hundred years later, the life of the Negro is still sadly crippled by the manacles of segregation and the chains of discrimination. One hundred years later, the Negro lives on a lonely island of poverty in the midst of a vast ocean of material prosperity. One hundred years later, the Negro is still languishing in the corners of American society and finds himself an exile in his own land. So we have come here today to dramatize a shameful condition... In a sense we have come to our nation's capital to cash a check. When the architects of our republic wrote the magnificent words of the Constitution and the Declaration of Independence, they were signing a promissory note to which every American was to fall heir. This note was a promise that all men, yes, black men as well as white men, would be guaranteed the unalienable rights of life, liberty, and the pursuit of happiness.... It is obvious today that America has defaulted on this promissory note insofar as her citizens of color are concerned. Instead of honoring this sacred obligation, America has given the Negro people a bad check, a check which has come back marked "insufficient funds." But we refuse to believe that the bank of justice is bankrupt.

Martin Luther King, Jr. (1963)

"I Have A Dream"

1

This nation owes the Negro $49,000,000,000.00
for work performed and services rendered.

Bishop Henry McNeil Turner (1893)

2

If I'm not the person you say that I am,
then you are not the person you think that you are.

James Baldwin

3

I am because WE are and, since WE are, therefore I am.

Proverb - South Africa

4

There is debt to the Negro people which America can never repay.
At least then, they must make amends.

Sojourner Truth

5

The roaring lion kills no prey.

Proverb - Nigeria

6

Every great dream begins with a dreamer. Always remember, you have within you the strength, the patience, and the passion to reach for the stars to change the world.

Harriet Tubman

7

Power conceded nothing without demand. It never did and it never will.

Frederick Douglass

8

God gives the hardest battles to the toughest soldiers.

Elder's Wisdom

9

It is thrifty to prepare today for the wants of tomorrow.

Aesop

10

Injustice anywhere is a threat to justice everywhere.

Rev. Martin Luther King, Jr., Ph.D.

11

As young African men and women, we have the power to change the quality of our lives. We have to educate ourselves, but not in the traditional public-school way, because the curriculum is not enough to fill the heart, soul and mind of a Black child. We have to use the libraries and spend time in bookstores looking for alternative forms of information. We need to make resources out of the elders in our communities!

Sista Souljah

12

If you do not spare a day to fix a door to your room, you will waste three years searching for your money, but you will never find it.

Proverb - Ghana

13

Indeed our survival and liberation depend upon our recognition of the truth when it is spoken and lived by the people. If we cannot recognize the truth, then it cannot liberate us from untruth. To know the truth is to appropriate it, for it is not mainly reflection and theory. Truth is divine action entering our lives and creating the human action of liberation.

James H. Cone, PH.D.

14

In all of God's Creation there is nothing more alluring, more appealing, or attractive; nothing more beautiful, more charismatic, more charming or captivating; nothing more delightful, more elegant, or exquisite; nothing more fascinating, more gorgeous, more inspiring, or intoxicating; nothing more magnificent or lovely than a Black woman's smile.

Ty Gray-EL

15

Freedom is a state of mind. It is the outgrowth of our willingness to make conscious choices of our own free will and to live through the consequences of our choices without blame, shame or guilt.

Iyanla Vanzant

16

What God puts in store for someone never goes rotten.

Proverb

17

Chance has never yet satisfied the hope of a suffering people. Action, self-reliance, the vision of self and the future have been the only means by which the oppressed have seen and realized the light of their own freedom.

Marcus Garvey

18

Every day may not be good... But there is something good in every day.

Elder's Wisdom

19

I don't trust people who don't love themselves and yet tell me, "I love you."

Maya Angelou

20

Authentic self (a knowledge of self rooted in truth) is the prerequisite for authentic relationships with others.

Lathardus Goggins II, Ed.D.

21

I had too much sense… I would never be any service to any one as a slave.. a mind like mine, restless, inquisitive and observant … The manner in which I learned to read and write, not only had great influence on my own mind … I had the greatest of confidence.

Nat Turner 1831

22

I did not know I was a slave until I found out
I couldn't do the things I wanted.

Frederick Douglass

23

We don't hate nobody because of their color. We hate oppression!

Bobby Seale

24

If you don't know where you're going, any direction will do.

Elder's Wisdom

25

When you run alone, you run fast. When you run together, you run far.

Proverb

26

It is not with saying, "Honey," "Honey,"
that sweetness will come into the mouth.

Proverb

27

Love is speech and/or action, that RESULTS in the use of TRUTH, in a manner that promotes the practice of JUSTICE and CORRECTNESS at all times, in all places, in all Nine Areas of People Activity: Economics, Education, Entertainment, Labor, Law, Politics, Religion, Sex and/or War.

Neely Fuller Jr.

28

Quarrels end, but words once spoken never die.

Proverb

29

To minimize the crimes of the Atlantic slave trade, which occurred from the fifteenth through the nineteenth century, by making racism everyone's disease, you make it incurable, something like bad weather, that one does not like but must put up with. We may bitch about racism, it may even be fashionable to be distressed about it, but nevertheless we must live with it.

Clarence J. Munford, Ph.D.

30

Excellence overcomes prejudice. The pursuit of excellence overcomes obstacles.

Capt. Roscoe Brown, Ph.D.

31

If you have come to help me, you are wasting your time. But if you have come because your liberation is bound up with mine, then let us work together.

Lilla Watson

SEPTEMBER

The history of a nation is, unfortunately, too easily written as the history of its dominant class. But if the history of a nation, or a people, cannot be found in the history of a class, how much less can the history of a continent be found in what is not even a part of it - Europe. Africa cannot be validly treated merely as the space in which Europe swelled up. If African history is interpreted in terms of the interests of European merchandise and capital, missionaries and administrators, it is no wonder that African nationalism is in the forms it takes regarded as a perversion and neo- colonialism as a virtue.

In the new African renaissance, we place great emphasis on the presentation of history. Our history needs to be written as the history of our society, not as the story of European adventures. African society must be treated as enjoying its own integrity; its history must be a mirror of that society, and the European contact must find its place in this history only as an African experience, even if as a crucial one. That is to say, the European contact needs to be assessed and judged from the point of view of the principles animating African society, and from the point of view of the harmony and progress of this society. When history is presented in this way, it can become not an account of how those African students referred to in the introduction became more Europeanized than others; it can become a map of the growing tragedy and the final triumph of our society. In this way, African history can come to guide and direct African action. African history can thus become a pointer at the ideology which should guide and direct African reconstruction.

Dr. Kwame Nkrumah (1964)
Consciencism: Philosophy and Ideology for Decolonisation

1

It is childish to remain in a hole when you can take yourself out.

Proverb

2

Science literacy is a vaccine against the charlatans of the world that would exploit your ignorance.

Neil deGrasse Tyson, Ph.D.

3

We have to give our children, especially black boys, something to lose. Children make foolish choices when they have nothing to lose.

Jawanza Kunjufu, Ed.D.

4

Sometimes when you point out the moon and stars, all they see is the tip of your finger.

Proverb - Sukuma (Tanzania)

5

Pan Africanists want Africa to face neither East nor West but forward. ... Pan Africanism's clarion call for over a century now, has been that Africans must get rid of their image of poverty and powerlessness. They must look inward. ... to throw away their slave and colonial mentality and bear the brunt of their own Pan African success in the same way they did during Africa's struggle against classical colonialism.

Motsoko Pheko, Ph.D.

6

Each one teach one.

Elder's Wisdom

7

Learning does not make one learned: there are those who have knowledge and those who have understanding. The first requires memory and the second philosophy.

Alexandre Dumas

8

What an old man sees sitting, a young man cannot see standing.

Proverb

9

Knowledge rooted in experience shapes what we value and as a consequence how we know what we know as well as how we use what we know.

bell hooks, Ph.D.

10

None but ourselves can free our minds.

Bob Marley

11

Knowledge is the key that unlocks all doors. It does not matter what you look like or where you come from if you have knowledge.

Benjamin Carson, M.D.

12

When a fool is cursed, he thinks he is being praised.

Proverb

13

If you are going to hold someone down, you're going to have to hold on to the other end of the chain. You are confined by your own system of oppression.

Toni Morrison

14

An African should not be made to suffer from a gunshots in Europe.

Proverb - Ghana

15

It is easier to build strong children than to repair broken men.

Frederick Douglass

16

Whether the knife falls on the melon or
the melon on the knife, the melon suffers.

Proverb

17

Powerful people cannot afford to educate the people that they oppress, because once you are educated you will not ask for power, you will take it!

John Henrik Clarke, Ph.D.

18

A cutting word is worse than a bowstring,
a cut may heal, but the cut of the tongue does not.

Proverb

19

There is nothing more attractive than a woman who carries herself like a queen and wears her confidence like a crown! Royalty or not, dignity and respect are every woman's birthright.

Khari Tourè

20

The fool speaks, the wise man listens.

Proverb

21

It is far better to be free to govern or misgovern yourself, than to be governed by anybody else.

Kwame Nkrumah, Ph.D.

22

To educate as the practice of freedom is a way of teaching that anyone can learn. That learning process comes easiest to those of us who teach who also believe that there is an aspect of our vocation that is sacred; who believe that our work is not merely to share information but to share in the intellectual and spiritual growth of our students. To teach in a manner that respects and cares for the souls of our students is essential if we are to provide the necessary conditions where learning can most deeply and intimately begin.

bell hooks, Ph.D.

23

A weapon which you don't have in your hand won't kill a snake.

Proverb

24

Education is the most powerful weapon
which you can use to change the world.

Nelson Mandela

25

He who learns, teaches.

Proverb

26

Our elevation must be the result of self-efforts and work of our own
hands. No other human power can accomplish it. If we but determine
it shall be so, it will be so.

Maj. Martin Delany

27

If the inexpressible cruelties of slavery could not stop us, the
opposition we now face will surely fail. We will win our freedom
because the sacred heritage of our nation and the eternal will of God
are embodied in our echoing demands.

Rev. Martin Luther King, Jr., PhD

28

Any river that forgets its source will definitely dry up.

Proverb

29

Understand that as a teacher you are working with a soul, which came from God, which belongs to God, and will eventually return to God. You will be held accountable.

Moses L. Osborne

30

Pray for what you need, but always work for what you want.

Proverb

OCTOBER

I loved the arts and sciences ... growing-up as a little girl and teenager, I loved designing doll clothes, and wanting to be a fashion designer. I took art and ceramics, and I loved to dance... Lola Falana, Alvin Ailey, Jerome Robbins. And, I avidly followed the Gemini and Apollo programs; I had science projects and tons of astronomy books. I took calculus and philosophy; I wondered about infinity and the big bang theory. ... The creativity that allowed us to conceive, build, and launch the Space Shuttle springs from the same source of imagination and analysis that it takes to carve a Bundu statue, or the ingenuity it took to design, choreograph, and stage Cry. ... The difference between science and the arts is not that they are different sides of the same coin even, or even different parts of the same continuum, but rather, they are manifestations of the same thing. The arts and sciences are avatars of human creativity. It's our attempt as human beings to build an understanding of the universe, the world around us. They are both apart of us.

Mae Jemison, M.D. (2002)
TED Conference

1

When you take a knife away from a child, give him a piece of wood instead.

Proverb - Kenya

2

History is a clock that people use to tell their time of day. It is a compass they use to find themselves on the map of human geography. It tells them where they are, and what they are.

John Henrik Clarke, Ph.D.

3

When you sort out the grains, it becomes pure.

Proverb - Tigrinya (Ethiopia)

4

The greatness of a man is not in how much wealth he acquires, but in his integrity and his ability to affect those around him positively.

Bob Marley

5

The forest though looks thick, when one approaches it,
one sees that each tree is on it's own.

Proverb - Akan (Ghana)

6

Education is our passport to the future, for tomorrow belongs to
the people who prepare for it today.

El-Hajj Malik El-Shabazz (Malcolm X)

7

Half education is more dangerous than no education.

Proverb

8

My hope emerges from those places of struggle where I witness
individuals positively transforming their lives and the world around
them. Educating is always a vocation rooted in hopefulness. As
teachers we believe that learning is possible, that nothing can keep an
open mind from seeking after knowledge and finding a way to know.

bell hooks, Ph.D.

9

Tomorrow is pregnant and no one knows what she will give birth to.

Proverb

10

We get closer to God as we get more intimately and understandingly acquainted with the things He has created. I know of nothing more inspiring than that of making discoveries for one's self.

George Washington Carver

11

An old broom sweeps clean... It knows all the corners of the house.

Elder's Wisdom

12

I've learned that people will forget what you said, people will forget what you did, but people will never forget how you made them feel.

Maya Angelou

13

An intelligent enemy is better than a stupid friend.

Proverb

14

There was not, no matter where one turned, any accepted image of oneself, no proof of one's existence. One had the choice, either of "acting just like a nigger" or of not acting just like a nigger - and only those who have tried it know how impossible it is to tell the difference.

James Baldwin

15

Never teach a child that their history begins with slavery.

Runoko Rashidi

16

Your beauty will take you there, but your character will bring you back.

Proverb

17

Never be limited by other people's limited imaginations. If you adopt their attitudes, then the possibility won't exist because you'll have already shut it out...You can hear other people's wisdom, but you've got to re-evaluate the world for yourself.

Mae Jemison, M.D.

18

Happiness is a perfume, you can't pour it on somebody else without getting a few drops on yourself.

James Van Der Zee

19

To know nothing is bad, to learn nothing is worse.

Proverb - Serer

20

If you have no confidence in self, you are twice defeated in the race of life. With confidence, you have won even before you have started.

Marcus Garvey

21

A person, who knows the use of proverbs, reconciles difficulties.

Proverb - Akan (Ghana)

22

Invest in the human soul. Who knows, it might be a diamond in the rough.

Mary McLeod-Bethune

23

It is the rainy season that gives wealth.

Proverb - Hausa

24

Every people should be originators of their own destiny.

Maj. Martin Delany

25

No amount of success can compensate for failure in the home!

Elder's Wisdom

26

I would now remind my beloved Black Sisters that a positive, optimistic loving woman strengthens and gives life to a man, but an antagonistic, negative or pessimistic one can destroy him. The same applies to brothers in relationship to sisters. Yet, in the final analysis, it is the woman who determines what type of treatment she will receive and accept from a man. She is the one who can ultimately inspire him to be a real man...

Ishakamusa Barashango

27

A bitter heart devours its owner.

Proverb - Herero

28

One of the greatest propaganda campaigns of all time was the masterful marketing of the myth of black inferiority to justify slavery within a democracy.

Tom Burrell

29

You do not embrace those who will take you straight to hell, no matter how much blood you share with them. ... And, most importantly, it is not healthy to keep the company of people who proudly wear the scars of the generations of their physical and mental rape.

Mwalimu Baruti

30

When somebody says, "The dead are happier than I am," let him remember that his time will come.

Proverb - Baya

31

From birth to death, the Negro is handled, distorted and violated by the symbols and tentacles of whites' powers, tentacles that worm their way into his neurons and invades the grey cells of his cortex... The Negro not only dons a mask; he becomes, in many instances, the mask he dons.

Lerone Bennett, Jr.

NOVEMBER

"Political organizations are formed to keep the powerful in power. Their first rule is "don't rock the boat." If someone makes trouble and you can get him, do it. If you can't get him, bring him in. Give him some of the action, let him have a taste of power. Power is all anyone wants, and if he has a promise of it as a reward for being good, he'll be good. Anyone who does not play by those rules is incomprehensible to most politicians."

Shirley Chisholm

1

It may take faith the size of a mustard seed to move a mountain, but you better bring your shovel.

> Douglas Goggins Sr.

2

Two birds disputed about a kernel,
when a third swooped down and carried it off.

> Proverb

3

I refuse to let my personal success ... explain away the injustices to fourteen million of my people. ... I flight for the right of the Negro people ... to have decent homes, decent jobs, and the dignity that belongs to every human being.

> Paul Robeson

4

A leader does not wish for war.

> Proverb - Kenya

5

There is a higher law than the law of government. That's the law of conscience.

Kwame Tourè (Stokely Carmichael)

6

Ninety-nine lies may help you, but the hundredth will give you away.

Proverb - Hausa

7

It is with our passions as it is with fire and water;

they are good servants, but bad masters.

Aesop

8

The end of an ox is beef, and the end of a lie is grief.

Proverb

9

Violence always rebounds, always returns home.

Lerone Bennett, Jr.

10

Before you go out with a widow, you must first ask her what killed the husband.

Proverb - Nigeria

11

A nation that continues year and year to spend more money on military defense than on programs of social uplift is approaching spiritual death.

Rev. Martin Luther King, Jr., PhD

12

In the South they don't care how close blacks get, as long as we don't get too high. In the North they don't care how high blacks get, as long as we don't get too close.

Elder's Wisdom

13

Dominator culture has tried to keep us all afraid, to make us choose safety instead of risk, sameness instead of diversity. Moving through that fear, finding out what connects us, reveling in our differences; this is the process that brings us closer, that gives us a world of shared values, of meaningful community.

bell hooks, Ph.D.

14

One does not have to learn how to fall into a pit; all it takes is the first step, the others take care of themselves.

Proverb - Wolof

15

A candid examination of race matters takes us to the core of the crisis of American democracy. And the degree to which race matters ... is a crucial measure of whether we can keep alive the best of this democratic experiment we call America.

Cornel West, Ph.D.

16

When a head is too big, it cannot avoid punches.

Proverb

17

Racism is so universal in this country, so widespread and deep-seated, that it is invisible because it is so normal.

Shirley Chisholm

18

God gives blessing to all people. If people had to distribute them, many would go without.

Proverb - Hausa

19

Don't lose your head in the game and keep your eyes on the prize.

Kindred the Family Soul

20

A man who suffers much, knows much; every day brings him new wisdom.

Proverb - Ewe

21

We demand every political right, privilege and position to which the whites are eligible in the United States, and we will either attain to these, or accept nothing.

Maj. Martin Delany

22

Courage is a decision you make to act in a way that works through your own fear for the greater good as opposed to pure self-interest. Courage means putting at risk your immediate self-interest for what you believe is right.

Derrick Bell

23

Let's put some purpose in this party.

Tom Joyner

24

Time is neutral and does not change things.
With courage and initiative, leaders change things.

Jesse Jackson, Sr.

25

You do not become a chief simply by sitting on a big stool.

Proverb - Akan (Ghana)

26

A government, which uses force to maintain its rule, teaches
the oppressed to use force to oppose it.

Nelson Mandela

27

It is better to know your own faults than those of your neighbor.

Proverb - Serer

28

If you are neutral in situations of injustice,
you have chosen the side of the oppressor.

Desmond Tutu

29

Agents of change don't see the world as it is, but how they dream it to be.

Cory Booker, J.D.

30

You don't make progress by standing on the sidelines, whimpering and
complaining. You make progress by implementing ideas.

Shirley Chisholm

100

DECEMBER

Obviously the African culture has had to sustain severe blows and may have been battered nearly out of shape by the belligerent cultures it collided with, yet in essence even today one can easily find the fundamental aspects of the pure African culture in the present day African. ... One of the most fundamental aspects of our culture is the importance we attach to Man. ... a Man-centered society ... the capacity we have for talking to each other-not for the sake of arriving at a particular conclusion but merely to enjoy the communication for its own sake. ... We regard our living together not as an unfortunate mishap warranting endless competition among us but as a deliberate act of God to make us a community of brothers and sisters jointly involved in the quest for a composite answer to the varied problems of life. ... Any suffering we experienced was made much more real by song and rhythm. There is no doubt that the so called 'Negro Spirituals' sung by black slaves in the States as they tiled under oppression were indicative of their African heritage. ... African society had the village community as its basis ... This obviously was a requirement to suit the needs of a community-based and man-centered society ... Africans do not recognize any cleavage between the natural and supernatural. They experience a situation rather than face a problem......More as a response of the total personality to the situation than the result of some mental exercise ... We thanked God through our ancestors before we drank beer, married, worked etc. We would obviously find it artificial to create special occasions for worship. God was always in communication with us and therefore merited attention everywhere and anywhere.

Steve Biko (1971)

I Write What I Like

1

When the blind lead the blind, both shall fall into the ditch. Proverb

2

Black awareness is the essential beginning step in creating a framework for understanding and accomplishing the educational and political work that values our humanity. Real empowerment begins by learning the lessons of our own heritage and knowing something about ourselves.

Manning Marable, Ph.D.

3

It's ain't where you're from, it's where you're at; even if you're from the ghetto.

Rakim

4

No one rises to low expectations.

Les Brown

5

The child that leaves the fate of his future in the hope of inheritance property, sets himself up for a life of poverty.

Proverb

6

The genius of our black foremothers and forefathers was ... to equip black folk with cultural armor to beat back the demons of hopelessness, meaninglessness, and lovelessness.

Cornel West, Ph.D.

7

No matter how far a stream flows, it never forgets it's source.

Proverb

8

To be a Negro in America... means fighting daily a double battle - a battle against pathology within and a battle against oppression without.

Rev. Martin Luther King, Jr., Ph.D.

9

Show me your friend and I will show you your character.

Proverb

10

Nobody's free until everybody's free.

Fannie Lou Hamer

11

The rain does not fall on one roof.

Proverb - Ewe

12

A person who doubts himself is like a man who would enlist in the ranks of his enemies and bear arms against himself. He makes his failure certain by himself being the first person to be convinced of it.

Alexandre Dumas

13

The educational system of a country is worthless unless it revolutionizes the social order. Men of scholarship, and prophetic insight, must show us the right way and lead us into light which is shining brighter and brighter.

Carter G. Woodson, Ph.D.

14

We have to talk about liberating minds as well as liberating society.

Angela Davis

15

I want there to be a place in the world where people can engage in one another's differences in a way that is redemptive, full of hope and possibility. Not this "In order to love you, I must make you something else". That's what domination is all about, that in order to be close to you, I must possess you, remake and recast you.

bell hooks, Ph.D.

16

The ruin of a nation begin in the homes of it's people.

Proverb   Ghana

17

We need God to bring insight to our sight.

Rev. Ronald J. Fowler

18

The basic tenet of Black consciousness is that the Black man must reject all value systems that seek to make him a foreigner in the country of his birth and reduce his basic human dignity.

Steve Biko

19

The first step toward tolerance is respect and
the first step toward respect is knowledge.

Henry Louis Gates, Jr., Ph.D.

20

If the elders leave you a legacy of dignified language,
you do not abandon it and speak childish language.

Proverb - Ghana

21

I pity the man who believes that he knows everything.

Runoko Rashidi

22

If there is no struggle, there is no progress.

Frederick Douglass

23

What is culture? It binds us to each other. It gives us identity. It gives us a reason for surviving; and it tells us who we should live for and who we should die for (if we have to). Culture is the energy source for thriving. It gives a sense of security. It also puts us in a system of accountability.

Marimba Ani, Ph.D.

24

Prejudice is learned. It's not a self-winding watch.

Muhammad Ali

25

Every race of people since time began who have attempted to describe God by words or painting, or by carvings, have conveyed their idea that the God who made them and shaped their destinies was symbolized in themselves...

Henry McNeal Turner

26

A weak person goes where he is smiled at.

Proverb - Herero

27

A people without the knowledge of their history, origin and culture is like tree without roots.

Marcus Garvey

28

The whitewashing of racism is often coupled with the view that Black people are subject to 'social sicknesses,' that we are the prey of 'psycho pathologies' variously called 'welfare sub-culture,' 'poverty syndrome,' 'pimping on poverty,' 'underclass desperation,' and such like. The academic psychological establishment insists that the terrible conditions endured in urban Black America are not due to racial discrimination, but rather to neutral causes like 'damaging childhood experiences,' 'familial disarray' and 'dysfunctions built into the sub-culture and self-perpetuating,' in the final analysis, always due to the nature of the 'Negro's racial soul.' The 'negro has himself to blame for his social predicament, but really he should not be blamed because it is in his unalterable nature to be inferior' -- the circle is closed."

Clarence J. Munford, Ph.D.

29

Keep the main thing the "main thing."

Lathardus Goggins, Ph.D., Ed.D., Ed.S.

30

Three things are important in this world: Good health, peace with one's neighbor, friendship with all.

Proverb - Serer

31

Sankofa - It is not taboo to go back and fetch what you forgot.

Proverb - Ghana

INDEX

For additional links to African-centered wisdom, scholarship, and cultural heritage visit

Baobab Virtual Reference Desk at

http://www.afrocentric.info/Baobab.

365 Black: Nuggets of Wisdom